First Field Trips

Concert

by Rebecca Pettiford

MIDLOTHIAN PUBLIC LIBRARY
14701 S. KENTON AVENUE
MIDLOTHIAN, IL 60445

Bullfrog Books

Ideas for Parents and Teachers

Bullfrog Books let children practice reading informational text at the earliest reading levels. Repetition, familiar words, and photo labels support early readers.

Before Reading

• Discuss the cover photo. What does it tell them?

• Look at the picture glossary together. Read and discuss the words.

Read the Book

• "Walk" through the book and look at the photos. Let the child ask questions. Point out the photo labels.

• Read the book to the child, or have him or her read independently.

After Reading

• Prompt the child to think more. Ask: Have you ever been to a concert? What did you hear? What kind of performance space was it held in?

Bullfrog Books are published by Jump!
5357 Penn Avenue South
Minneapolis, MN 55419
www.jumplibrary.com

Copyright © 2016 Jump! International copyright reserved in all countries. No part of this book may be reproduced in any form without written permission from the publisher.

Library of Congress Cataloging-in-Publication Data

Pettiford, Rebecca.
  Concert / by Rebecca Pettiford.
    pages cm. — (First field trips)
  Includes index.
  ISBN 978-1-62031-294-0 (hardcover: alk. paper) —
  ISBN 978-1-62496-360-5 (ebook)
  1. Concerts—Juvenile literature.
  2. School field trips—Juvenile literature. I. Title.
  ML3928.P47 2016
  780.78—dc23
                                    2015030638

Editor: Jenny Fretland VanVoorst
Series Designer: Ellen Huber
Book Designer: Lindaanne Donohoe
Photo Researcher: Lindaanne Donohoe

Photo Credits: All photos by Shutterstock except: Alamy, 16–17; Igor Bulgarin/Shutterstock, 6–7, 22; iStock, 4, 5, 19; Martin Good/Shutterstock.com, 10–11, 13; PhotoHouse/Shutterstock.com, 18–19; testing/Shutterstock.com, 14–15; Thinkstock, 8, 12.

Printed in the United States of America at Corporate Graphics in North Mankato, Minnesota.

Table of Contents

Listen Up!

Our class is on a field trip.

We are at a concert.

What happens at a concert?
People make music.

Some people play instruments.
They are musicians.

Some people sing.

They are singers.

We go to
a music hall.

Shh! It's time
to be quiet.

The conductor
is here.

What does he do?

He directs the musicians.

He waves a stick.

stick

12

conductor

They watch him.
They begin to play.

There are all kinds
of concerts.

Sometimes people
dance.

They play drums.

Boom! Boom!

Sometimes people sing.
They are in a choir.

We go to a park.
A band plays music.
Wow! It is great!

The music stops.

We clap.

The concert was fun.

Let's go again soon!

At the Music Hall

instruments

musicians

conductor

singer

Picture Glossary

band
A group of musicians.

concert
A live music show.

choir
A group of people who sing.

field trip
A trip students take to learn about something.

Index

To Learn More

Learning more is as easy as 1, 2, 3.

1) Go to www.factsurfer.com

2) Enter "concert" into the search box.

3) Click the "Surf" button to see a list of websites.

With factsurfer.com, finding more information is just a click away.